Contents

Articles

References

Hull City A.F.C.

Hull City A.F.C.

Full name	Hull City Association Football Club
Nickname(s)	The Tigers
Founded	1904
Ground	KC Stadium, Hull, East Riding of Yorkshire (Capacity: 25,404)
Chairman	Russell Bartlett
Manager	Nigel Pearson
League	The Championship
2009–10	Premier League, 19th (relegated)

Home colours	Away colours

⚽ *Current season*

Hull City Association Football Club is an English football club based in Kingston upon Hull, East Riding of Yorkshire, founded in 1904. They play in the Football League Championship. In 2007–08 they achieved promotion to the top flight of English football for the first time in their history, by winning the Championship play-off final at Wembley Stadium. They finished the 2008–09 season 17th in the Premier League table, successfully avoiding relegation by one point. The previous highest position Hull City had finished in the English Football League was third in the old second division in 1909–10, which they matched in 2007–08 when they gained promotion. Their greatest achievement in cup competitions came in 1930, when the team reached the semi-finals of the FA Cup.

Hull play their home games at the KC Stadium. They previously played at Boothferry Park, but moved to their current home in 2002, with Boothferry Park set for demolition. They traditionally play in black and amber, often with a striped shirt design, hence their nickname *The Tigers*. The club's mascot is

East Riding Of Yorkshire Football Clubs, including: Hull City A.f.c., North Ferriby United A.f.c., Bridlington Town A.f.c., Hall Road Rangers F.c., Goole A.f.c.

Hephaestus Books

Roary the Tiger.

History

Hull City Association Football Club was founded in June 1904. For some years previously, attempts had been made to found a football club, but this proved difficult because the city was then dominated by rugby league teams such as Hull FC and Hull KR.

Hull City's first season as a professional football club consisted only of friendly matches; because of the date of its founding, the club was unable to apply for membership of The Football League for the 1904–05 season. These early matches were played at The Boulevard, the home of rugby league club Hull FC. On 1 September 1904, Hull's debut match took place against Notts County; with 6,000 in attendance at The Boulevard, Hull held County to a 2–2 draw.

Hull's first competitive football match was in the FA Cup, but they were eliminated, after a replay, in the preliminary round against Stockton, the score was 7–4 on aggregate. After disputes with landlords at The Boulevard, Hull City moved to Anlaby Road Cricket Ground. After having played 44 friendly fixtures the previous season, Hull City were finally admitted into the Football League Second Division for the 1905–06 season. Other teams competing in the league that season included the likes of Manchester United and Chelsea, as well as Yorkshire rivals Leeds City, Bradford City and Barnsley. Hull faced Barnsley in their first game, a fixture which Hull won 4–1. Eventually, Hull would finish the season in fifth place.

The following season a new ground was built for Hull City across the road from the cricket ground. Still under the managership of Ambrose Langley, Hull continued to finish consistently in the top half of the table. They came close to promotion in the 1909–10 season, recording what would be their highest finish until they matched it in 2008. Hull finished third, level on points with second placed Oldham Athletic, missing promotion on goal average by 0.29 of a goal. Hull regularly finished in the top half of the table prior to the First World War, but after the war the team finished in the bottom half in seven seasons out of eleven, culminating in relegation to the Third Division North in 1930.

Mid-20th century

Hull's greatest achievement in cup competitions was in 1930, when they reached the FA Cup semi-finals. The cup run saw Hull knock out the eventual champions of the Second and Third Divisions; Blackpool and Plymouth Argyle respectively. They then knocked out Manchester City, to meet Newcastle United in the quarter finals. The first leg at St James' Park finished as a 1–1 draw, but in the replay Hull beat Newcastle 1–0. The semi-final match against Arsenal took place at Elland Road in Leeds, the game ended 2–2, and was taken to a replay. Arsenal knocked Hull out at Aston Villa's home ground, the game ending 1–0.

After the Second World War, the club moved to another new ground, Boothferry Park. In the 1948–49 season, managed by former England international Raich Carter, Hull won the Third Division North. "Yo-yoing" between the second and third tiers of English football, Hull City had promotion seasons from the Third to the Second Division again in 1959 and 1966, winning the Third Division in the latter season. Hull also became the first team in the world to go out of a cup competition on penalties, beaten by Manchester United in the semi-final of the Watney Mann Invitation Cup on 1 August 1970. By the early 1980s, Hull City were in the Fourth Division, and financial collapse led to receivership.

Don Robinson took over as chairman and appointed Colin Appleton as the new manager. Both had previously held the equivalent roles with non-league Scarborough. Promotion to Division Three followed in 1983, with a young team featuring the likes of future England international Brian Marwood, future England manager Steve McClaren, centre-forward Billy Whitehurst, and the prolific goal-scorer Les Mutrie. When Hull City missed out on promotion by one goal the following season, Appleton left to manage Swansea City.

Decline in the late 20th century

Hull reached the Second Division in 1986 under player-manager Brian Horton. They remained there for the next five years before finally going down in 1991, by which time the club's manager was Terry Dolan. Hull finished 14th in the Third Division in the 1991–92 season, meaning that they would be competing in the new Football League Division Two the following season. In their first season in the rebranded division, Hull narrowly avoided another relegation, but the board kept faith in Dolan and over the next two seasons they achieved several mid-table finishes. Financial difficulties hampered City's progress, as key players such as Dean Windass and Andy Payton had to be sold to fend off winding-up orders. In the 1995–96 season Hull were relegated to Division Three.

In 1997 the club was purchased by former tennis player David Lloyd, who sacked Dolan as manager and replaced him with Mark Hateley after Hull could only finish in 17th place in the table. Hull's league form was steadily deteriorating to the point that relegation to the Football Conference was looking a real possibility. Lloyd sold the club in November 1998 to a South Yorkshire based consortium, but retained ownership of Boothferry Park. Hateley departed in November 1998, with the club at the foot of the table. He was replaced by 34-year-old veteran player Warren Joyce, who steered the club to safety with games to spare. Hull City fans refer to this season as "The Great Escape". Despite this feat, Joyce was replaced in April 2000 by the more experienced Brian Little.

Boothferry Park in March 2008

Despite briefly being locked out of Boothferry Park by bailiffs and facing the possibility of liquidation, Hull qualified for the Division Three playoffs in the 2000–01 season, losing in the semi-finals. A boardroom takeover by former Leeds United commercial director Adam Pearson had eased the club's precarious financial situation and all fears of closure were banished.

The 21st century

Up the Football League

The new chairman ploughed funds into the club, allowing Little to rebuild the team. Hull occupied the Division Three promotion and playoff places for much of the 2001–02 season, but Little departed two months before the end of the season and Hull slipped to 11th under his successor Jan Mølby.

Hull began the 2002–03 season with a number of defeats, which saw relegation look more likely than promotion, and Mølby was sacked in October as Hull languished fifth from bottom in the league. Peter Taylor was named as Hull's new manager and in December 2002, just two months after his appointment, Hull relocated to the new 25,400-seater Kingston Communications Stadium after 56 years at Boothferry Park.. At the end of the season Hull finished 13th.

Wembley Stadium before the Championship play-off final against Bristol City

Hull were Division Three runners-up in 2003–04 and League One runners-up in 2004–05. These back-to-back promotions took them into the Championship, the second tier of English football. The 2005–06 season, the club's first back in the second tier, saw Hull finish in 18th place, 10 points clear of relegation and their highest league finish for 16 years.

However, Taylor left the club on 13 June 2006 to take up the manager's job at Crystal Palace. Phil Parkinson was confirmed as his replacement on 29 June 2006, but was sacked on 4 December 2006 with Hull in the relegation zone, despite having spent over £2 million on players. Phil Brown took over as caretaker manager, and took over permanently in January 2007, having taken Hull out of the relegation zone. Brown brought veteran striker Dean Windass back to his hometown club on loan from Bradford City, and his eight goals helped secure Hull's Championship status as they finished in 21st place. At the end of the season, former manager Brian Horton rejoined the club as Phil Brown's assistant.

Adam Pearson sold the club to a consortium led by Paul Duffen in June 2007, stating that he "had taken the club as far as I could", and would have to relinquish control in order to attract "really significant finance into the club". He resigned from the board on 31 July 2007, thus severing all ties with the club.

Under Paul Duffen and manager Phil Brown, Hull City improved greatly on their relegation battle of 2006–07 and qualified for the play-offs after finishing the season in third place. They beat Watford 6–1 on aggregate in the semi-finals and played Bristol City in the final on 24 May 2008, which Hull won 1–0 at Wembley Stadium, with Hull native Dean Windass scoring the winning goal. Their ascent from the bottom division of the English Football League to the top in just five seasons is the third-fastest ever.

Phil Brown and players celebrate on promotion to the Premier League in 2008

Top flight football

Despite being one of the favourites for relegation in the 2008–09 season, Hull began life in the Premier League by beating Fulham 2–1 on the opening day in their first ever top flight fixture. With only one defeat in their opening nine games, Hull City found themselves (temporarily) joint top of the table, third on goal difference, following a 3–0 victory over West Bromwich Albion – ten years previously they had been bottom of tier four of the league. Hull City's form never replicated the highs of the early autumn, winning only two more games over the remainder of the season. Despite the drop in form and slow slide down the table, Hull City went into the final game of the season in 17th place and above the drop zone. They ultimately lost the game against Manchester United 0–1, however Newcastle United and Middlesbrough also lost their games against Aston Villa and West Ham United respectively, thus securing a second Premier League season for Hull City.

On 10 June 2009, Hull City were officially announced as part of the Barclays Asia Trophy 2009. In this 4-team tournament Hull City competed against two other English sides, Tottenham Hotspur and West Ham United, as well as local side Beijing Guoan, who they beat 5–4 in a penalty shoot out after a 1–1 draw. On 31 July 2009, Hull City faced Tottenham Hotspur in the final of the Barclays Asia Trophy and were defeated 3–0. On 6 August 2009, Hull City acquired hotshot American international striker Jozy Altidore on loan from Spanish side Villarreal, with an option to buy him after the 2009–10 season.

On 29 October 2009 chairman Paul Duffen resigned his position with the club and was replaced by former chairman Adam Pearson on 2 November 2009 and on 15 March 2010 manager Phil Brown was relieved of his duties after a run of four defeats left Hull in the relegation zone. Brown's replacement was former Crystal Palace and Charlton boss, Iain Dowie and the appointment was met with some disbelief by supporters who were hoping for a "bigger name" replacement. Dowie's first move as manager was to bring Tim Flowers and Steve Wigley onto his backroom staff, with former Hull City manager Brian Horton joining Phil Brown on gardening leave.

Return to the Football League

Hull City's relegation from the Premier League was confirmed on 3 May 2010, after a 2–2 draw at Wigan Athletic. On 3 June, season tickets for the club's 2010–11 season in the Football League Championship went on general release sale. After relegation, the club handed over their share on Friday, 4 June. Phil Brown's contract as manager was confirmed ended on 7 June 2010, and the search for his replacement was to continue past mid-June as the club confirmed that Iain Dowie would ultimately not be retained in a managerial capacity. Nigel Pearson was confirmed as the new manager on 29 June, lured from Leicester City in part by the Championship ambitions of the Tigers. Perceived lack of support at the Midlands club and permission to bring along staffers Craig Shakespeare and Steve Walsh from the Foxes helped seal the deal. A reported block on player transfers into the club, set in place by the Hull City board on 28 July 2010 until transfers out substantially reduce the £39 million-per-year wage bill, at first cast doubt on the new manager's efforts to build a squad capable of a quick return to the Premier League; nevertheless, Pearson has since brought several transfers and loan signings into the club in his bid to strengthen the squad for the season's campaign.

Colours and crest

For most of the club's history, Hull have worn black and amber shirts with black shorts. These black and amber colours are where Hull's nickname, *The Tigers*, originated from. However, in the club's first match against Notts County in 1904, white shirts were worn, with black shorts and black socks. During their first season in the League, Hull wore black and amber striped shirts and black shorts, which they continued to wear until the Second World War with the exception of one season, in which they wore sky blue shirts. Following the end of the Second World War, Hull spent another season wearing sky blue, but changed to plain amber shirts, which they wore until the early 1960s, when they swapped back to stripes.

Original kit colours

During the mid 1970s and early 1980s, the strip was constantly changing between the two versions of plain shirts and stripes. During the late 1980s, red was added to the kits but its duration went no further than this. The early 1990s featured two "tiger skin" designs, which have since featured in several articles listing the "worst ever" football kits. The 1998–99 season introduced a kit with cross-fading amber and white stripes, another experiment that proved unpopular. After the turn of the century, the club wore plain amber shirts until 2004, when the club celebrated its centenary by wearing a kit similar to the design of the one worn 100 years ago.

Hull City did not wear a crest on their team shirts until 1947. This crest depicted a tiger's head in an orange-shaded badge, which was worn up until 1955, when it was changed to just the tiger's head. This was worn for four years, when the shirt again featured no emblem. Then, in 1971, the club returned to showing the tiger's head on the shirt. This was used for four years, until the club's initials of HCAFC were shown for five years. After this, a logo with the tiger's head with the club's name underneath was used from 1980 until 1998. The next logo, which as of 2009 is the club's current logo, features the tiger's head in an amber shield with the club's name, along with the club's nickname, *The Tigers*.

Stadium

Main articles: The Boulevard (stadium), Anlaby Road, Boothferry Park, and KC Stadium

Between 1904 and 1905, Hull City played their home games at The Boulevard. This ground was used by Hull on a contract which allowed them to use it when not used for Rugby League, at a cost of £100 per annum. Hull built their own ground, Anlaby Road, which was opened in 1906. With the threat of the rerouting of the railway line through the Anlaby Road ground, the club was convinced it needed to secure its future by owning its own ground. They negotiated the deal for land between Boothferry Road and North Road in 1929, which was financed by a £3,000 loan from the FA. Due to the club's financial difficulties, no work took place for three years, and development then stopped until 1939. In that year a

The KC Stadium

proposal to build a new multi-purpose sports stadium on the site temporarily halted the club's plans to relocate, but when this plan failed the club resolved to continue with the stalled development of the site, in anticipation of moving to the new stadium in 1940. The outbreak of war, however, meant that the redevelopment again came to a halt, as the site was taken over by the Home Guard.

During the Second World War, Anlaby Road was damaged by enemy bombing, the repair cost of which was in the region of £1,000. The Cricket Club served notice to quit at the same time, and so in 1943 the tenancy was officially ended. Hull were forced to return to the Boulevard Ground from 1944 until 1945 because of the poor condition of the planned stadium at Boothferry Road. The new stadium was finally opened under the revised name of Boothferry Park on 31 August 1946.

Hull City, along with one of the city's rugby league sides, Hull FC, moved into the newly-built KC Stadium in 2002. The KC Stadium was named "Best Ground" at the 2006 Football League Awards.

Statistics and records

For more details on this topic, see Hull City A.F.C. records.

Andy Davidson holds the record for Hull City league appearances, having played 520 matches. George Maddison comes second, having played 430 matches. Chris Chilton is the club's top goalscorer with 222 goals in all competitions. Chilton also holds the club record for goals scored in the League (193), FA Cup (16) and League Cup (10).

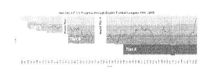

Chart showing the progress of Hull City A.F.C. through the English Football League system since joining in 1905–1906 to 2008–09

The club's widest victory margin in the league was their 11–1 win against Carlisle United in Division Three in 1939. Their heaviest defeat in the league was 8–0 against Wolves in 1911.

Hull City's record home attendance is 55,019, for a match against Manchester United on 26 February 1949 at Boothferry Park, with their highest attendance at their current stadium, the KC Stadium, 25,030 set on 9 May 2010 against Liverpool for the last match of the season.

The highest transfer fee received for a Hull City player is £4 million from Sunderland for Michael Turner. The highest transfer fee paid for a player is £5 million, for Jimmy Bullard from Fulham in January 2009.

Players

As of 1 October 2010

Current squad

Note: Flags indicate national team as has been defined under FIFA eligibility rules. Players may hold more than one non-FIFA nationality.

No.		Position	Player
1		GK	Matt Duke
2		DF	Kamil Zayatte
3		DF	Andy Dawson
4		MF	Ian Ashbee *(captain)*
5		DF	Paul McShane
7		MF	Richard Garcia
8		MF	James Harper
9		FW	Caleb Folan

No.		Position	Player
10		FW	Craig Fagan
11		MF	Kevin Kilbane
12		MF	John Bostock *(on loan from Tottenham Hotspur)*
13		GK	Mark Oxley
14		MF	Tom Cairney
16		MF	Péter Halmosi

No.		Position	Player
17		DF	Liam Cooper
18		MF	Nick Barmby
19		MF	Will Atkinson
20		MF	Jamie Devitt
21		FW	Mark Cullen
22		MF	Robert Koren
23		FW	Jay Simpson
24		MF	Nolberto Solano
25		DF	Anthony Gerrard *(on loan from Cardiff City)*
26		DF	Daniel Ayala *(on loan from Liverpool)*
27		MF	Jimmy Bullard
28		FW	Rowan Vine *(on loan from Queens Park Rangers)*
—		MF	Nicky Featherstone
—		DF	Steve Gardner

Out on loan

Note: Flags indicate national team as has been defined under FIFA eligibility rules. Players may hold more than one non-FIFA nationality.

No.		Position	Player
6		DF	Anthony Gardner *(at Crystal Palace until January 2011)*
15		MF	Seyi Olofinjana *(at Cardiff City until the end of the 2010–11 season)*
—		MF	Kamel Ghilas *(at AC Arles-Avignon until the end of the 2010–11 season)*

Player of the Year

Michael Turner, Player
of the year 2007–08,
2008–09

Year	Winner
2000–01	Ian Goodison
2001–02	Gary Alexander
2002–03	Stuart Elliott
2003–04	Damien Delaney
2004–05	Stuart Elliott
2005–06	Boaz Myhill
2006–07	Andy Dawson

2007–08	+ Michael Turner
2008–09	+ Michael Turner
2009–10	▓ ▓ Stephen Hunt

Managers

As of 2 October 2010

Only professional, competitive matches are counted.

Name	Nat	Managerial Tenure	G	W	D	L	Win %
James Ramster	+	August 1904 – April 1905	0	0	0	0	00.00
Ambrose Langley	+	April 1905 – April 1913	318	143	67	108	44.96
Harry Chapman	+	April 1913 – September 1914	45	20	10	15	44.44
Fred Stringer	+	September 1914 – July 1916	43	22	6	15	51.16
David Menzies	+	July 1916 – June 1921	90	31	27	32	34.44
Percy Lewis	+	July 1921 – January 1923	71	27	18	26	38.02
Billy McCracken	–⊢	February 1923 – May 1931	375	134	104	137	35.73
Haydn Green	+	May 1931 – March 1934	123	61	24	38	49.59
Jack Hill	+	March 1934 – January 1936	77	24	15	38	31.16
David Menzies	+	February 1936 – October 1936	24	5	8	11	20.83
Ernest Blackburn	+	December 1936 – January 1946	117	50	31	36	42.73
Frank Buckley	+	May 1946 – March 1948	80	33	19	28	41.25
Raich Carter	+	March 1948 – September 1951	157	74	41	42	47.13
Bob Jackson	+	June 1952 – March 1955	123	42	26	55	34.14
Bob Brocklebank	⧾	March 1955 – May 1961	302	113	71	118	37.41
Cliff Britton	+	July 1961 – November 1969	406	170	101	135	41.87
Terry Neill	–⊢	June 1970 – September 1974	174	61	55	58	35.05
John Kaye	+	September 1974 – October 1977	126	40	40	46	31.74
Bobby Collins	✕	October 1977 – February 1978	19	4	7	8	21.05
Ken Houghton	+	April 1978 – December 1979	72	23	22	27	31.94
Mike Smith	+	December 1979 – March 1982	99	27	29	43	27.27
Bobby Brown	✕	March 1982 – June 1982	19	10	4	5	52.63

Colin Appleton	┿	June 1982 – May 1984	91	47	29	15	51.64
Brian Horton	┿	June 1984 – April 1988	195	77	58	60	39.48
Eddie Gray	⤬	June 1988 – May 1989	51	13	14	24	25.49
Colin Appleton	┿	May 1989 – October 1989	16	1	8	7	6.25
Stan Ternent	┿	November 1989 – January 1991	62	19	15	28	30.64
Terry Dolan	┿	January 1991 – July 1997	322	99	96	127	30.74
Mark Hateley	┿	July 1997 – November 1998	76	17	14	45	22.36
Warren Joyce	┿	November 1998 – April 2000	86	33	25	28	38.37
Billy Russell*	⤬	April 2000 – April 2000	2	0	0	2	00.00
Brian Little	┿	April 2000 – February 2002	97	41	28	28	42.26
Billy Russell*	⤬	February 2002 – April 2002	7	1	1	5	14.29
Jan Mølby	▦	April 2002 – October 2002	17	2	8	7	11.76
Billy Russell*	⤬	October 2002 – October 2002	1	1	0	0	100.00
Peter Taylor	┿	October 2002 – June 2006	184	77	50	57	41.84
Phil Parkinson	┿	June 2006 – December 2006	24	5	6	13	20.83
Phil Brown	┿	December 2006 – June 2010	157	52	40	65	33.12
Iain Dowie†	┼	March 2010 – June 2010	9	1	3	5	11.11
Nigel Pearson	┿	June 2010–Present	11	3	3	5	27.27

* Caretaker manager

† Temporary Football Management Consultant

Current staff

As of 30 September 2010.

Position	Staff
Chairman	Russell Bartlett
Chief Executive	Mark Maguire
Head Of Football Operations	Adam Pearson
Manager	Nigel Pearson
Assistant Manager/First Team Coach	Craig Shakespeare

Assistant Manager/Head of Recruitment	Steve Walsh
Goalkeeping Coach	Mark Prudhoe
Development Coach	Stuart Watkiss
Fitness Coordinator	Sean Rush
Head of Youth	Billy Russell
Youth Recruitment Officer	Neil Mann
Head Physiotherapist	Simon Maltby
Assistant Physiotherapist	Liam McGarry
Youth Team Physiotherapist	Duncan Robson

Related teams

Reserves and Juniors

Main article: Hull City A.F.C. Reserves and Academy

Hull City Reserves play in the Premier Reserves League North Division. The team plays home fixtures at the Church Road Ground, home of North Ferriby United.

In the 2006–07 season, Hull finished in fourth place in the league table after picking up 31 points from their 18 league meetings. They also reached the semi-final of the League Cup before losing 3–2 to Hartlepool United Reserves.

Hull City Juniors play in the Football League Youth Alliance, playing their home fixtures at Winterton Rangers' home stadium. The juniors won the league title in the 2006–07 season by a 10 point margin, and retained the championship in the 2007–08 season, when they also won the Football League Youth Alliance Cup.

Hull City Women

Main article: Hull City Women A.F.C.

Hull City Women play in the Northern Combination Women's Football League. In the 2006–07 season, the team finished seventh in the table with 33 points.

Rivalries

According to a 2003 poll, Hull City fans consider their main rival to be Leeds United, although this is not reciprocated. Other rivals include their neighbours from across the Humber, Scunthorpe United and Grimsby Town. With Scunthorpe's promotion from League One, the 2007–08 Championship season saw the return of the "Humber Derby". Additionally Lincoln City and York City name Hull amongst their rivals. Lincoln City had an excellent record over Hull City, only losing once against the Tigers in the 21st century. Lincoln were also the first team to record an away win at Hull City's KC Stadium with a 1–0 victory in the 2002–03 season. The

Hull City supporters at the celebrations on the team's promotion to the Premier League in 2008

club also has a traditional rivalry with Sheffield United. In 1984 Sheffield United won promotion at Hull City's expense with the teams level on points and goal difference and separated only by goals scored, with 33 of United's goals scored by former Hull City striker Keith Edwards. City's final game of the season against Burnley had been rescheduled due to bad weather and took place after their promotion rivals had finished their campaign; Hull went into the game knowing that a three-goal victory would mean promotion, but in front of a crowd which included a number of United fans could manage only a 2–0 win, ensuring that Sheffield went up instead.

Honours

Honour	Year(s)
Football League Championship play-off winners	2007–08
Football League One Runners-up	2004–05
Football League Third Division Champions	1965–66
Football League Division Three Runners-up	2003–04
Football League Third Division Promoted	1984–85
Football League Third Division North Champions	1932–33, 1948–49

Football League Third Division North Runners-up	1958–59
Football League Fourth Division Runners-up	1982–83

See also

- Hull City Psychos
- Hull City A.F.C. seasons

External links

- Official club site [1]
- Hull City News – Sky Sports [2]
- Hull City A.F.C. on BBC Sport: Club News [3] – Recent results [4] – Upcoming fixtures [5] – Club stats [6]
- City Independent – a totally independent Fanzine and forum [7]
- Amber Nectar – long standing fanzine site and forum [8]
- Hull City Online – the original independent Tigers site [9]
- historicalkits.co.uk [10]
- HullCityPics.com [11]

North Ferriby United A.F.C.

North Ferriby United A.F.C.

Full name	North Ferriby United Association Football Club
Nickname(s)	The Villagers
Founded	1934
Ground	Grange Lane [1], Church Road, North Ferriby, East Riding of Yorkshire (Capacity: 2,700)
Chairman	⊣⊢ Les Hare
Manager	⊣⊢ Neil Allison
League	NPL Premier Division
2009-10	NPL Premier Division, 4th

Home colours	Away colours

North Ferriby United A.F.C. is a football club based in North Ferriby, near Kingston upon Hull, in the East Riding of Yorkshire, England. They were formed in 1934. They reached the Northern Premier League Premier Division for the first time in 2005. They won the Northern Premier League Division One title in 2005.

History

North Ferriby United was formed in 1934 as a result of a village meeting during which it was decided that it would be a good idea to form a local football team. They first took part in the local East Riding Church League and, in 1938, they won the Division One title.

The club was re-formed after the Second World War and were admitted to the East Riding Amateur League. The immediate post war years proved to be very successful with the highlight being an appearance in the final qualifying round of the FA Amateur Cup during the 1949-50 campaign.

In 1969, North Ferriby improved their status when they joined Division Two of the Yorkshire League: the following season they captured the championship and also lifted the East Riding Senior Cup. The year 1975 saw them win the Yorkshire League Cup by defeating Lincoln United 2-0. Twelve months later they finished second to Emley in Division One.

The 1970s were a very positive period for the club and saw them win the East Riding Senior Cup three times. They reached the lofty heights of the FA Cup Third Qualifying Round stage in the 1980/81 season, where they lost away to Boston United.

In 1982 they joined the newly formed Northern Counties East League, finishing as runners-up in Division One North. Promotion to the Premier Division was offered to them but had to be declined because the ground facilities were not up to the required standard.

The 1985-86 season saw them take the Division One title and this time they were promoted. They also reached the Fourth Round Proper of the FA Vase and the following year went out in the Fifth Round to Farsley Celtic by 2-1.

Three seasons later national recognition came their way when they advanced to the semi-final of the FA Vase losing to Tamworth, after just shading the first leg at Tamworth 2-1.

In 1991, North Ferriby United won the inaugural President's Cup, defeating FA Vase champions Guiseley 8-5 on aggregate. They also lifted the East Riding Senior Cup for the first time in twelve years and in the League Cup Final they lost 1-0 to Guiseley. The 1996-97 season saw them achieve the ambition of every non-League club when they appeared in the FA Vase Final at Wembley Stadium. A 3-1 aggregate victory over Guisborough Town in the semi-final saw them through to the FA Carlsberg Vase Final at Wembley Stadium on Saturday 19 May 1997. A 3-0 defeat by Whitby Town only partially marred their great day and their name is now proudly entered in the record books.

Northern Premier League

The next two seasons saw them miss promotion to the Northern Premier League but in 1999-2000 season they won the Northern Counties East League Championship and, with all the necessary work having been carried out to the ground, they finally achieved their long time goal of promotion to the higher level of non-League football.

The first season saw the club set a new post-war record by lifting the East Riding Senior Cup for a fifth successive season.

The 2001-02 season was the club's second season in the Northern Premier League and the club's progression continued with a higher League placing. The campaign finished on another high as the club retained the East Riding Senior Cup for a sixth year in succession, thus equalling the all-time record held by Hull City in a period which straddled the Second World War. The following season the club gained a place in the Promotion Play-Offs via fourth place in the table. Although the promotion push floundered on a tense evening at Radcliffe Borough, that disappointment was assuaged by the club taking the outright record from Hull City with a seventh successive East Riding Senior Cup triumph.

The 70th Anniversary Season, 2004-05, proved to be one of the most rewarding in the club's history as the young team clinched the First Division Championship on the final day of the season at Mossley. The side led the division from early October and, despite a minor slump in March, never relinquished their grip on top spot.

Last season saw the club at the highest level in their history as they entered the Premier Division and led the table from the off until March. Despite missing out on automatic promotion, the club came close to joining Champions Blyth Spartans in the Conference North as they secured a place in the promotion play-offs thanks to a fifth place finish. They defeated third placed Frickley Athletic away from home on penalty kicks before losing the final by the odd goal in three at Farsley Celtic after extra time.

Players

As of 25 November 2009.

Current squad

Note: Flags indicate national team as has been defined under FIFA eligibility rules. Players may hold more than one non-FIFA nationality.

No.		Position	Player
—	+	GK	Steve Wilson
—	+	GK	Ben Hallam
—	+	DF	Tom Matthews
—	+	DF	Ryan Levesley
—	+	DF	Kevin Larvin
—	+	DF	Paul Ellender
—	+	DF	Sam Denton
—	+	DF	Paul Foot
—	+	MF	Paul Harsley

No.		Position	Player
—	+	MF	Wayne Brooksby
—	+	MF	James Williams
—	+	MF	Chris Bolder
—	+	MF	Russell Fry
—	+	MF	Chris White
—	+	MF	Peter Davidson
—	+	FW	Gary Bradshaw
—	+	FW	Alex Davidson
—	+	FW	Gareth Owen

Notable former players

- + Dean Windass
- + Leo Fortune-West

Non Playing Staff

Chairman: Les Hare

Vice-Chairman: Colin Wicks

Secretary: Steve Tather

Press Officer and Historian: Philip Withers

Programme Editor: Richard Watts

Manager: Neil Allison

Assistant Manager: John Anderson

Physio: Martin Woodmansey

Club Captain: Paul Foot

Honours

League

- **NPL Premier Division**
  - **Play-Off Finalists (1):** 2005–06
- **NPL Division One**
  - **Winners (1):** 2004–05
  - **Play-Off Semi-Finalists (1):** 2002–03
- **NCEL Premier Division**
  - **Winners (1):** 1999–00
  - **Runners-Up (1):** 1997–98
  - **Third-Placed (3):** 1986–87, 1992–93, 1995–96
- **NCEL Division One**
  - **Winners (1):** 1985–86
- **NCEL Division One (North)**
  - **Runners-Up (1):** 1982–83
- **YFL Division One**
  - **Runners-Up (1):** 1975–76
  - **Third-Placed (2):** 1978–79, 1980–81
- **YFL Division Two**
  - **Winners (1):** 1970–71
  - **Third-Placed (2):** 1969–70, 1973–74

Cup

- **FA Vase**
  - **Runners-Up (1):** 1996–97
- **NCEL Presidents Cup**
  - **Winners (3):** 1990–91, 1998–99, 1999–2000
- **East Riding Senior Cup**
  - **Winners (16):** 1970–71, 1976–77, 1977–78, 1978–79, 1990–91, 1996–97, 1997–98, 1998–99, 1999–2000, 2000–01, 2001–02, 2002–03, 2006–07, 2007–08, 2008–09, 2009–10

External links

- Official site [2]

Bridlington Town A.F.C.

Bridlington Town A.F.C.

Full name	Bridlington Town Association Football Club
Nickname(s)	Seasiders Town
Founded	1918 as Bridlington Central United (*reformed 1994*)
Ground	Queensgate [1], Bridlington, East Riding of Yorkshire (Capacity: 3,000 (740 seated))
Chairman	╬ Peter Smurthwaite
Managers	╬ Gary Allanson
League	Northern Counties East League Premier Division
2009-10	NCEL Premier Division, 1st

Home colours	Away colours

Bridlington Town A.F.C. are an English football club, based in Bridlington, in the East Riding of Yorkshire. They were founded in 1918 and currently play in the Northern Counties East League Premier Division. The club's reserve team play in the Humber Premier League.

History

The club was founded in 1918 as **Bridlington Central United** after World War I. The team joined the Driffield and District Minor League, soon joinging the Driffield and District League. After several seasons of hard work, the team were promoted into the East Riding Amateur League, they won the championship five consecutive times during the 1950s. They also won the East Riding Senior Cup twice around this time.

Yorkshire League

The club changed their name to **Bridlington Town F.C.** in 1959 and moved into the Yorkshire League Division Two, during their first season in that league, they finished runners up and were promoted. In 1960-61 they reached the First Round proper of the FA Cup eventually losing out to Bishop Auckland who were very strong at the time.

In the mid to late 1960s, Town built up a rivalry with fellow Bridlington side Bridlington Trinity. During the 1966-67 season in the Yorkshire League, Town won the championship while Trinity finished second. The following year it would be Trinity who took the title and Town finished in third. This rivalry continued until the early 1970s when Trinity became part of the Midland League.

Northern Counties East League

In 1982 the club were one of the founder members of the Northern Counties East League after the Yorkshire and Midland Leagues were merged. They were put into Northern Counties East League Division One, here they stayed for four seasons.

By 1986-87, they were promoted to the Northern Counties East League Premier Division, even though they only finished sixth. This was because several teams in the Premier Division had resigned in the close season. This gave Town the opportunity to ignite their old rivalry with Bridlington Trinity, for the first time since the early 1970s.

During the first three seasons in the Premier Division, Town finished higher. With a third and a fourth place, while Trinity were in the bottom half. The 1989-90 season was the concluding showdown for the two clubs. Town were crowned champions, while Trinity ended the season a respectable fourth. This would prove to be the end of the rivalry as Trinity folded due to the termination of their groundshare with Bridlington Town. Unfortunately for Bridlington, they were unable to put the icing on the cake in their FA Vase final clash at Wembley with Yeading, they drew the game, but lost in the replay 1-0 at Elland Road.

Cup and League success, before folding

Ken Richardson had joined the club as President and was essential in helping the club with the necessary finance to develop their ground, in order to climb the football ladder. They added a new stand, clubhouse, turnstiles and floodlights.

Town marched on to the Northern Premier League Division One. The 1992-93 season was the most successful in the clubs history, they finished as champions of the NPL Division One, and they finally took the FA Vase at Wembley, beating Tiverton Town 1-0. Alan Radford scored the only goal of the game.

The sunny spell would not last, due to legalities, the team were forced to play their home games at Doncaster Rovers' ground; Belle Vue. The club went into turmoil. They finished 21st in the Northern

Premier League Premier Division and were deducted three points. Instead of going into Northern Premier League Division One, they folded.

Return

A local pub team **The Greyhound**, approached the lease-holders of Bridlington Town's former stadium Queensgate, looking for it to become their base. A deal was struck under the condition that the team would change their name to **Bridlington Town AFC**, essentially bringing the old club back to the town.

The Greyhound club agreed and a new club crest was designed and a new motto *"Pergere et Eniti"*, which means *"Onwards and Upwards"*. The club returned on 10 September 1994, and were put into the league where they had originally played during their formative years; the Driffield and District League, it was literally back to square one.

Bridlington progressed steadily, gaining entry to the East Riding County League Division One, they won the league and cup double. After three seasons in the East Riding County League Premier Division, Town finished runners-up and applied for promotion back into the Northern Counties East League Division One. They were accepted and spent three seasons at this level; finishing fifth, and then fourth, before achieving promotion with a runners-up spot in 2001-02.

Town made their mark in 2002-03, reaching the quarter-final of the FA Vase before going out to Brigg Town. And they also reached the Fourth Qualifying Round of the FA Cup, eventually losing to Conference National side Southport. Bridlington Town won the league that year, they were crowned champions with 20 points ahead of the runners-up.

Recent times

The club were back in the Northern Premier League Division One and focused all their attention on it. Bridlington Town finished eleventh but were promoted back into the Northern Premier League Premier Division after the league was re-organised. Amazingly in 10 years after they were forced to start again, the club had pulled themselves back up to the highest division they had been in. It took the original club 85 years to reach that level.

In 2007, it was announced that Bridlington Town would play in the inaugural season of the Northern Premier League Division One North. However a disastrous campaign followed, and they finished bottom of the division, and were relegated to the Northern Counties East League Premier Division.

Honours

- **Northern Premier League First Division**
  - Champions: 1992-93
- **NCEL Premier Division**
  - Champions: 1989-90, 2002-03, 2009-10
- **NCEL Division One**
  - Runners-up: 2001-02
  - Promoted: 1985-86
- **Yorkshire League**
  - Champions: 1966-67
- **Yorkshire League Division Two**
  - Champions: 1974-75
  - Runners-up: 1959-60
- **FA Vase**
  - Winners: 1992-93
  - Runners-up: 1989-90

Records

- **FA Cup**
  - First Round: defeated 3-2 by Bishop Auckland in 1960-61 and defeated 2-1 by York City in 1991-92.
- **FA Trophy**
  - Second Round Replay: defeated 4-0 by Eastwood Town in 2004-05.

External links

- Highlights from the FA Cup Extra Preliminary round on ITV Local Yorkshire - Bridlington v Guisborough 16 August 2008 [2]
- Official site from 2006 [3]
- Official site to 2005-06 [4]
- Un official fans forum [5]

Hall Road Rangers F.C.

Hall Road Rangers F.C.

Full name	Hall Road Rangers Football Club
Nickname(s)	*Rangers*
Founded	1959
Ground	Dene Park Dunswell, Hull (Capacity: 1200 (*250 seats*))
Chairman	Robert Smailes
Manager	Martin Thacker
League	Northern Counties East League Premier Division
2009-10	Northern Counties East League Premier Division, 11th

Home colours	**Away colours**

Hall Road Rangers Football Club is an English football club formed in 1959. They play their games at Dene Park in the village of Dunswell in the East Riding of Yorkshire, four miles north of Hull.

History

The club was formed in 1959 by a local man named Ted Richardson, Hall Road Rangers was originally set-up as a youth club for young teenagers and played Sunday league football. The club became a senior team and stepped up into the Yorkshire Football League Division Two in 1968. In 1970, they were placed in the newly formed Division 3. Hall Road won the Division 3 title in 1973. They were relegated back to Division 3 in 1976. Division 3 champions again in 1980.

Hall Road Rangers were founding members of the Northern Counties East League in 1982. They were placed in Division 1 North, but finished bottom that first season. They spent the 1983-84 season in Division 2 North, but a league reshuffle saw Hall Road return to Division 1 North for 1984-85. Further league reshuffles saw Hall Road in division 3 in 1985-86 and Division 2 in 1986-87, where they stayed until 1991 when they won the Division 2 title. The NCEL scrapped Division 2 that year so the entire division moved up to Division 1. For the 2007-08 season, they were members of Northern Counties East League Division One. They finished the season as runners up, thereby gaining promotion to the Premier Division.

Hall Road won the East Riding Senior Cup in 1973 and 1994. They also won the Wilkinson Sword Trophy in 2004.

External links

- Official website [1]

Geographical coordinates: 53°47′52.51″N 0°22′00.80″W

Goole A.F.C.

Goole A.F.C.

Full name	Goole AFC
Nickname(s)	The Vikings
Founded	1912 (Goole Town) 1997 (Goole AFC)
Ground	Victoria Pleasure Grounds [1] , Goole (Capacity: 3,000 (300 seated))
Chairman	Chris Hoff
Manager	Karl Rose
League	Northern Premier League Division One South
2009-10	Northern Premier League Division One South, 18th

Home colours	Away colours

Goole AFC is a semi-professional English football club based in the town of Goole, East Riding of Yorkshire, founded in 1912. They currently compete in the Northern Premier League Division One South, which is at Step 4 on the football pyramid.

The club has spent its entire existence in non-league football to date, where they have won various championships over the years. Perhaps Goole's crowning achievement so far was reaching the FA Cup third round in 1956-57 before going out to Nottingham Forest.

History

The club was founded in 1912 as **Goole Town Football Club** when they entered into the Midland Football League. Town played in that league for three seasons, finishing each season respectably and with a highest position of 4th place in 1914-15. That same season they reached the First Round of the FA Cup, but lost to Middlesbrough 9-3 at Ayresome Park.

Play was suspended because of the First World War and Goole did not re-enter the Midland League afterwards. However, just after the war, as **Goole Shipyards Football Club** they became founding members of the Yorkshire Football League for the 1920-21 season.

In 1924 the club had reverted to the Goole Town name and were back in the Yorkshire League. By the late 1920s Goole had proved themselves at this level, their pinnacle in this period being their championship-winning season in 1927-28. Goole continued in the Yorkshire League throughout the 1930s and 1940s, picking up the championship during both the 1936-37 and 1947-48 seasons.

Return to the Midland League

In 1948, Goole Town decided to return to the Midland Football League, which they had not competed in since the start of the First World War. At the end of 1950-51, they finished in 3rd place above the likes of Peterborough United and Boston United.

For the rest of the 1950s however, Goole lingered in the lower regions of the league, but had one very notable FA Cup run. In the 1956-57 season Goole Town reached the Third Round of the FA Cup, having previously knocked out Wigan Athletic 2-1 away and Football League Third Division North side Workington, before finally going out to Nottingham Forest.

The 1960s for Goole Town was largely uneventful in the league; the majority of the time they finished around mid-table, with a decent 5th place finish in 1967-68 being the highlight. That season they had also taken Spennymoor United to a first round replay in the FA Cup.

Northern Premier League

Goole Town became one of the founding members of the Northern Premier League in 1968, where they played against the likes of Macclesfield Town, Scarborough and Stafford Rangers - alongside old rivals Boston United and Wigan Athletic. During the first-ever season of the league, they finished in 8th place.

Their best finish in the Northern Premier League was 6th place on two occasions these were the 1976-77 season and then again in the 1988-89 season, while their worst finishes were in 1970-71, 1985-86 and 1992-93 seasons when they finished in last place on each occasion.

They reached the quarterfinal of the FA Trophy in the 1974-75 season, losing at home to Matlock Town 1-0 before a crowd of 3,500.

The club folded at the end of the 1995-96 season due to financial difficulties.

Goole AFC: 1997 - present

Goole AFC was formed in its place during 1997, though the club is generally seen as an official continuation of their predecessor{fact}.

Recently the club have been successful, having become champions of the Northern Counties East League in 2005 and are currently playing in the Northern Premier League Division One.A re-organisation of the non-league structure during the summer of 2006 saved them from an immediate return to the Northern Counties East League, as they finished in the relegation places at the end of the 2005-06 season.

The 2006-07 season saw a major upturn in form, with a 7th place finish earned after collecting just 5 less points than was needed to reach the play-offs, and 2007-08 was much the same with Goole missing out on the play-offs again after a faltering last quarter to the season.

In 2008-09 Goole AFC started the season on -10 points for entering Administration.

Goole's best season in the FA Vase was getting to the 4th Round in 1998-99, where they lost 0-1 to Bemerton Heath Harlequins in front of a crowd of 592.

Recent events

The club announced that they had changed their name to *Goole Town F.C.* in June 2006, however the West Riding FA rejected the name change thus forcing them to remain as Goole AFC.

Just before the start of the 2008-09 season it was announced that Goole AFC have an unpaid bill of £30,000 to HM Revenue and Customs, which issued a Winding-Up Notice on 17 July 2008. Goole AFC decided to enter into Administration to enable a CVA to agreed with HM Revenue and Customs. In the 2008–09 season, Goole AFC were deducted 11 points (-1 for an illegible player and -10 points for going into Administration.)

Prior to the 2009/10 season Goole AFC enticed Leo Fortune West to the VPG, the 38-year-old is expected to give the forward line a boost for the new season.

Due to a very poor start to the 2009-10 season which saw the club throw away large leads in games, lose heavily in the FA CUP and lose players such as Fortune-West, the management team of Nigel Danby and Mick Norbury resigned from their positions at the club; according to local press reports if they did not resign they would have been sacked. Journeyman Karl Rose replaced Nigel Danby as manager.

On Thursday 10th June 2010, Goole AFC announced that Des O'Hearne had resigned as Chairman and Chris Hoff would succeed him with immediate effect

Current squad

Note: Flags indicate national team as has been defined under FIFA eligibility rules. Players may hold more than one non-FIFA nationality.

No.	Position	Player
	GK	Craig Parry
	GK	Jamie Ward
	GK	Tom Osbourne
	DF	Chris Fawcus
	DF	Lee Stratford
	DF	Adam Green
	DF	James Dudgeon
	DF	Luke Jeffs
	DF	Sam Beard
	DF	Brett Lovell

No.	Position	Player
	MF	Terry Barwick
	MF	Daz Winter
	MF	Glyn Cotton
	MF	Steve Wilkinson
	MF	Luke Fletcher
	MF	Rory Prendergast
	MF	Lawrence Hunter
	FW	Gavin Allott
	FW	Mickey Goddard
	FW	Ashley Worsfold
	FW	Adam Lee
	FW	Billy Law

Notable former Goole AFC players

- Leigh Jenkinson
- Clint Marcelle
- Andy Saville
- Andy Flounders
- Clive Freeman
- Jason Blunt
- Gary Bradshaw
- Mick Norbury

Notable former Goole Town FC Players

- Tony Galvin
- Tony Currie
- Terry Curran
- Dave Rushbury
- Tibor Szabo
- Ricardo Gabbiadini
- Dave Burr
- Stewart Mell
- Paul Showler
- Norman Hallam

Records

- Goole AFC's top attendance in any game since formation was against a Leeds United side in 1999, when 976 turned up to watch Leeds win the game 5-3.
- Goole AFC's top attendance for a competitive game was against FC United of Manchester in the Unibond President's Cup Semi-Final in 2008 when 967 fans turn out, FC United of Manchester won the game 3-1. This was also the largest competitive attendance since 1987 when Goole Town lost to Nuneaton Borough in the FA Cup the attendance that day been 868.
- Goole Town's top attendance in any game was against Scunthorpe United in the 1949-50 season, when 8,700 packed into the VPG for this important league match.
- The largest crowd in recent years was when Manchester United played a friendly against Goole Town in March 1987, the match which Manchester United narrowly won 4-3 was watched by 1,759 supporters.
- The largest league crowds in recent years was a 2-0 defeat against Barrow when 786 turned up, a few weeks earlier Goole Town beat Witton Albion 3-0 in front of 730 supporters.

Biggest Wins

- Goole AFC's biggest win came in their very first competitive game when they beat Blackwell Miners Welfare 8-0.
- Goole AFC's biggest Northern Premier League win was against Kidsgrove Athletic when they won 6-2 in 2008

Ground and Colours

They play their home games at the ageing Victoria Pleasure Grounds ("VPG"). Plans to upgrade the VPG to Football Conference standards are being put together at the time of writing. Although an option is available to move the club to the proposed new Westfield Banks Sports Academy, which will enable the local Council to sell the VPG and put funds into the new venture.

The team's colours are red shirts, with red shorts and red socks. The away colours are yellow shirts, with yellow shorts and yellow socks.

Honours

- **Yorkshire League**
  - Winners: 1927-28, 1936-37, 1947-48, 1949-50
  - Runners-up: 1948-49
- **Yorkshire League Division Two**
  - Runners-up: 1932-33
- **Northern Premier League Cup**
  - Winners: 1988-89
  - Runners-up: 1984-85
- **Northern Counties East League Premier Division**
  - Winners: 2004-05
- **Northern Counties East League Division One**
  - Winners: 1999-00
- **Northern Counties East League Wilkinson Sword Trophy**
  - Winners: 1999-00
- **Central Midlands League Supreme Division**
  - Promoted 1998-99
- **Central Midlands League Premier Division**
  - Winners: 1997-98

- **West Riding County Cup**
  - Winners: 1951, 1952, 1957, 1969, 1970, 1976, 1977, 1978, 1985, 1987, 1989, 1992, 2007

External links

- Official Goole AFC Website [2]
- Goole Town/AFC History Website [3] Not complete

Article Sources and Contributors

Hull City A.F.C. *Source*: http://en.wikipedia.org/?oldid=390180620 *Contributors*:

North Ferriby United A.F.C. *Source*: http://en.wikipedia.org/?oldid=387581847 *Contributors*: Pedanticjohn

Bridlington Town A.F.C. *Source*: http://en.wikipedia.org/?oldid=378805737 *Contributors*: Keith D

Hall Road Rangers F.C. *Source*: http://en.wikipedia.org/?oldid=360932342 *Contributors*: 1 anonymous edits

Goole A.F.C. *Source*: http://en.wikipedia.org/?oldid=385726978 *Contributors*: 1 anonymous edits

Image Sources, Licenses and Contributors

Lightning Source UK Ltd.
Milton Keynes UK
UKOW05f0722081115

262275UK00008B/89/P